A
LITTLE WHITE SHADOW

BY

Mary Ruefle (signature)

So much the less complete
. . . .

First Edition

WAVE BOOKS
Seattle & New York
2006

Published by Wave Books
www.wavepoetry.com

Copyright © 2006 by Mary Ruefle

Library of Congress Control Number: 2005936629

Printed in Canada

Wave Books 004

A Little White Shadow.

—

one in ruins

struck

notes   whose sounds

spent a winter here

The

number

blue,

encircled herself

autumn

had no particular talents but   genius.

he

quickly

spoke fluently in many languages,

a human humming bird

the

island   drifted into

Dante

the shadows   growing longer and more purple

seven centuries of

sobbing

gathered
in the

twilight.

and

had their

pages

wandered,   through

the   dead.

borrow so little from
the past

as if they were alive,

It
was my duty to keep
the   piano   filled with roses.

We really did

like   Bohemia

, and the little

winds blowing

on rainy days,

and art was and would always

be

and her hair, well it might grow

white in time
would always

come for me

and grow confidential

then
curve her shoulders
and

say something philosophic.
that
evaporated
like the rivers in a Chinese picture

other people   read

sonnets

but

my cousin Suvia

never cared for

blood

, and in this as in

most things I agreed with her.

I had been

sketching

tall pink

heather,

her hat being the only thing moving

I was brought in contact
with the phenomenon peculiar to
"A   shadow."

its

. Everyone you met
was sure, sooner or later, to speak

the

time,—

No one at the Villa

made me
secretly think of children chasing butterflies.

the flapping white

dresses of the fish

rising sharply against the sky

at last standing breathless before

two donkeys

stopped and spoke with them.

the servant

seemed to be a

lady in   quaint
de Medici costume,

resting on soft
red cushions,   partially
covered with   hands

my

ignorance.

was a refining influence

the view from the window
stopped

and said, " Here I lie day after
day and

and the only things I possess
which can travel, can go no farther,

think me

lazy

always idle; but

my brain

grows weary   just thinking how to make

thought,

very simply,

"It's always noon with me.

pale, and
deformed but very interesting,

"

sorrows of

a little Quietist,

it was she was not known beyond her own little

I think what will always lin-
ger longest in our memories of her

we never would any of us
miss

suffering

would lay back
on her pillows exhausted with the intensity of

hope

a heart
a heart when
laden hearts
cause they

showed me a little book

saints

disagreed with her.

artists

and their quarrels .

a barbarity worthy of the Goths themselves.

flowers and birds

not able

to say
something practical about human companionship

. the

pen

was   going to try and join us there later,
provided the fever did not break out

the last
three years had taken no vacation,

and the

world seemed

drowsy

on the German piano.

birds were singiug

in the language

which some
believe he wrote after he drew the portrait of her

in black velvet

the last one
he wrote when quite an old man

Ren-
dered into English

this was something of its meaning:

paper
on
fire

They had been at a loss for a subject
at first, but had finally chosen

look-
ing down the road as if waiting for

a new volume of Browning

I could not bear to say good bye.   never
seemed to have held anything so hard   be-
fore.

                    went away without   word
for fear of breaking   Yet in the hall I turned

the shadows were pattering and

the bells of the Angelus were ringing and the

Our Lady of

shadowy boats

three weeks later

brought us news of

September

married very quietly to
Rome

on her way back to Russia,

Agnes,   Agnes,

the stern sad problems of human

existence

has its pauses

having once caught

sight of

a letter

God

changed .

the "Little

White Shadow"

END

on   end